If found, please return to:

How do I use this book?

Every time someone observes you teach, simply hand them this book, smile, and ask them to leave you some feedback.

How will it make me better?

This book is full of templates carefully designed to make sure you get consistent, balanced and manageable feedback.

It will help you keep all your feedback in one place, so you, and those supporting you, can see how your practice is evolving over time.

If you have suggestions for how this book could be improved, please do get in touch. I'm deeply passionate about this stuff and would love to hear from you.

And if this book has helped you, spread the word. Tell your colleagues, write a blog-post, and if you're feeling particularly generous, leave a quick one-line review on Amazon.

Cheers!

Peps
E: pepsmccrea@gmail.com
T: @pepsmccrea

Class details	Date & time
Observer	Focus

Commentary

Turn to the back for tips on leaving great feedback

continued...

Strengths

Suggestions

Class details	Date & time
Observer	Focus

Commentary

Turn to the back for tips on leaving great feedback

continued...

Strengths

Suggestions

Turn to the back for tips on leaving great feedback

Class details	Date & time
Observer	Focus

Commentary

Turn to the back for tips on leaving great feedback

continued...

Strengths

Suggestions

Turn to the back for tips on leaving great feedback

Class details	Date & time
Observer	Focus

Commentary

Turn to the back for tips on leaving great feedback

continued...

Strengths

Suggestions

Turn to the back for tips on leaving great feedback

Class details	Date & time
Observer	Focus

Commentary

Turn to the back for tips on leaving great feedback

continued...

Strengths

Suggestions

Turn to the back for tips on leaving great feedback

Class details	Date & time
Observer	Focus

Commentary

Turn to the back for tips on leaving great feedback

continued...

Strengths

Suggestions

Turn to the back for tips on leaving great feedback

Class details	Date & time
Observer	Focus

Commentary

Turn to the back for tips on leaving great feedback

continued...

Strengths

Suggestions

Turn to the back for tips on leaving great feedback

Class details	Date & time
Observer	Focus

Commentary

Turn to the back for tips on leaving great feedback

continued...

Strengths

Suggestions

Turn to the back for tips on leaving great feedback

Class details	Date & time
Observer	Focus

Commentary

Turn to the back for tips on leaving great feedback

continued...

Strengths

Suggestions

Turn to the back for tips on leaving great feedback

Class details	Date & time
Observer	Focus

Commentary

Turn to the back for tips on leaving great feedback

continued...

Strengths

Suggestions

Turn to the back for tips on leaving great feedback

Class details	Date & time
Observer	Focus

Commentary

Turn to the back for tips on leaving great feedback

continued...

Strengths

Suggestions

Turn to the back for tips on leaving great feedback

Class details	Date & time
Observer	Focus

Commentary

Turn to the back for tips on leaving great feedback

continued...

Strengths

Suggestions

Turn to the back for tips on leaving great feedback

Class details	Date & time
Observer	Focus

Commentary

Turn to the back for tips on leaving great feedback

continued...

Strengths

Suggestions

Turn to the back for tips on leaving great feedback

Class details	Date & time
Observer	Focus

Commentary

Turn to the back for tips on leaving great feedback

continued...

Strengths

Suggestions

Turn to the back for tips on leaving great feedback

Class details	Date & time
Observer	Focus

Commentary

Turn to the back for tips on leaving great feedback

continued...

Strengths

Suggestions

Turn to the back for tips on leaving great feedback

Class details	Date & time
Observer	Focus

Commentary

Turn to the back for tips on leaving great feedback

continued...

Strengths

Suggestions

Turn to the back for tips on leaving great feedback

Class details	Date & time
Observer	Focus

Commentary

Turn to the back for tips on leaving great feedback

continued...

Strengths

Suggestions

Turn to the back for tips on leaving great feedback

Class details	Date & time
Observer	Focus

Commentary

Turn to the back for tips on leaving great feedback

continued...

Strengths

Suggestions

Turn to the back for tips on leaving great feedback

Class details	Date & time
Observer	Focus

Commentary

Turn to the back for tips on leaving great feedback

continued...

Strengths

Suggestions

Turn to the back for tips on leaving great feedback

Class details	Date & time
Observer	Focus

Commentary

Turn to the back for tips on leaving great feedback

continued...

Strengths

Suggestions

Turn to the back for tips on leaving great feedback

Class details	Date & time
Observer	Focus

Commentary

Turn to the back for tips on leaving great feedback

continued...

Strengths

Suggestions

Turn to the back for tips on leaving great feedback

Class details	Date & time
Observer	Focus

Commentary

Turn to the back for tips on leaving great feedback

continued...

Strengths

Suggestions

Turn to the back for tips on leaving great feedback

Class details	Date & time
Observer	Focus

Commentary

Turn to the back for tips on leaving great feedback

continued...

Strengths

Suggestions

Turn to the back for tips on leaving great feedback

Class details	Date & time
Observer	Focus

Commentary

Turn to the back for tips on leaving great feedback

continued...

Strengths

Suggestions

Turn to the back for tips on leaving great feedback

Class details	Date & time
Observer	Focus

Commentary

Turn to the back for tips on leaving great feedback

continued...

Strengths

Suggestions

Turn to the back for tips on leaving great feedback

Class details	Date & time
Observer	Focus

Commentary

Turn to the back for tips on leaving great feedback

continued...

Strengths

Suggestions

Turn to the back for tips on leaving great feedback

Class details	Date & time
Observer	Focus

Commentary

Turn to the back for tips on leaving great feedback

continued...

Strengths

Suggestions

Turn to the back for tips on leaving great feedback

Class details	Date & time
Observer	Focus

Commentary

Turn to the back for tips on leaving great feedback

continued...

Strengths

Suggestions

Class details	Date & time
Observer	Focus

Commentary

Turn to the back for tips on leaving great feedback

continued...

Strengths

Suggestions

Turn to the back for tips on leaving great feedback

Class details	Date & time
Observer	Focus

Commentary

continued...

Strengths

Suggestions

Turn to the back for tips on leaving great feedback

Class details	Date & time
Observer	Focus

Commentary

Turn to the back for tips on leaving great feedback

continued...

Strengths

Suggestions

Turn to the back for tips on leaving great feedback

Class details	Date & time
Observer	Focus

Commentary

Turn to the back for tips on leaving great feedback

continued...

Strengths

Suggestions

Turn to the back for tips on leaving great feedback

Class details	Date & time
Observer	Focus

Commentary

continued...

Strengths

Suggestions

Turn to the back for tips on leaving great feedback

Class details	Date & time
Observer	Focus

Commentary

Turn to the back for tips on leaving great feedback

continued...

Strengths

Suggestions

Turn to the back for tips on leaving great feedback

Class details	Date & time
Observer	Focus

Commentary

Turn to the back for tips on leaving great feedback

continued...

Strengths

Suggestions

Class details	Date & time
Observer	Focus

Commentary

Turn to the back for tips on leaving great feedback

continued...

Strengths

Suggestions

Turn to the back for tips on leaving great feedback

Class details	Date & time
Observer	Focus

Commentary

Turn to the back for tips on leaving great feedback

continued...

Strengths

Suggestions

Turn to the back for tips on leaving great feedback

Class details	Date & time
Observer	Focus

Commentary

continued...

Strengths

Suggestions

Turn to the back for tips on leaving great feedback

Class details	Date & time
Observer	Focus

Commentary

Turn to the back for tips on leaving great feedback

continued...

Strengths

Suggestions

Turn to the back for tips on leaving great feedback

Class details	Date & time
Observer	Focus

Commentary

Turn to the back for tips on leaving great feedback

continued...

Strengths

Suggestions

Class details	Date & time
Observer	Focus

Commentary

Turn to the back for tips on leaving great feedback

continued...

Strengths

Suggestions

Turn to the back for tips on leaving great feedback

Class details	Date & time
Observer	Focus

Commentary

continued...

Strengths

Suggestions

Class details	Date & time
Observer	Focus

Commentary

continued...

Strengths

Suggestions

Turn to the back for tips on leaving great feedback

Class details	Date & time
Observer	Focus

Commentary

Turn to the back for tips on leaving great feedback

continued...

Strengths

Suggestions

Turn to the back for tips on leaving great feedback

Class details	Date & time
Observer	Focus

Commentary

Turn to the back for tips on leaving great feedback

continued...

Strengths

Suggestions

Turn to the back for tips on leaving great feedback

Class details	Date & time
Observer	Focus

Commentary

Turn to the back for tips on leaving great feedback

continued...

Strengths

Suggestions

Turn to the back for tips on leaving great feedback

Class details	Date & time
Observer	Focus

Commentary

Turn to the back for tips on leaving great feedback

continued...

Strengths

Suggestions

Class details	Date & time
Observer	Focus

Commentary

Turn to the back for tips on leaving great feedback

continued...

Strengths

Suggestions

Turn to the back for tips on leaving great feedback

Class details	Date & time
Observer	Focus

Commentary

Turn to the back for tips on leaving great feedback

continued...

Strengths

Suggestions

Turn to the back for tips on leaving great feedback

Class details	Date & time
Observer	Focus

Commentary

Turn to the back for tips on leaving great feedback

continued...

Strengths

Suggestions

Turn to the back for tips on leaving great feedback

About Peps

Peps Mccrea is an award-winning teacher educator, author and edtech entrepreneur.

He is a Senior Lecturer in Teacher Education at a large University in the UK, and co-founder of edtech startups Staffrm and Numeracy Ready.

Peps has three Masters degrees, two small kids, and dances like no one is watching, which is probably for the best.

Visit **pepsmccrea.com** for the full shebang.

Lean
Lesson
Planning

A practical approach to doing less and achieving more in the classroom

Peps Mccrea

Great feedback is

Balanced — The best feedback identifies things that someone is doing well (and so should *keep* doing), as well as things that could move them forward.

Focusssed — The best feedback focuses on a few important things (three or less) - things that will lead to the greatest gains.

Coherent — The best feedback takes account of previous feedback. Before you write, have a flick back through previous pages, and try to craft your feedback as part of the bigger picture.

Sensitive — The best feedback takes into account the delicate nature of being observed. It focuses on events and behaviours (things that can be changed) rather than personal characteristics.

Actionable — The best feedback is written in a way that allows people to put it into action the next time they step into a classroom. Supplement your suggestions with examples for extra oomph.

Printed in Great Britain
by Amazon.co.uk, Ltd.,
Marston Gate.